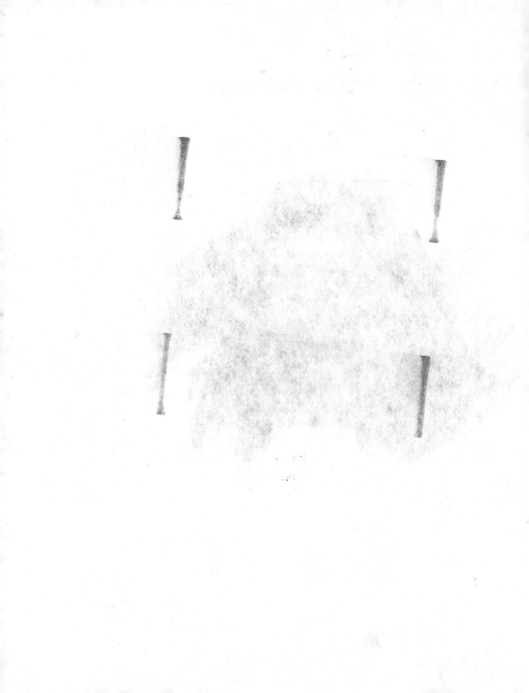

SandCastle 3

Punctuation

Exclamation Point

Mary Elizabeth Salzmann

Publishing Company

Published by SandCastle™, an imprint of ABDO Publishing Company, 4940 Viking Drive, Edina, Minnesota 55435.

Printed in the United States.

Photo credits: Eyewire Images, PhotoDisc

Library of Congress Cataloging-in-Publication Data

Salzmann, Mary Elizabeth, 1968-
    Exclamation point / Mary Elizabeth Salzmann.
       p. cm. -- (Punctuation)
    Includes index.
    ISBN 1-57765-621-0
    1. English language--Punctuation--Juvenile literature. 2. English language--Exclamations--Juvenile literature. [1. English language--Punctuation. 2. English language--Exclamations.] I. Title.

PE1450 .S26 2001
428.2--dc21

                                                        2001033020

The SandCastle concept, content, and reading method have been reviewed and approved by a national advisory board including literacy specialists, librarians, elementary school teachers, early childhood education professionals, and parents.

Let Us Know

After reading the book, SandCastle would like you to tell us your stories about reading. What is your favorite page? Was there something hard that you needed help with? Share the ups and downs of learning to read. We want to hear from you! To get posted on the ABDO Publishing Company Web site, send us email at:

sandcastle@abdopub.com

About SandCastle™

Nonfiction books for the beginning reader

- Basic concepts of phonics are incorporated with integrated language methods of reading instruction. Most words are short, and phrases, letter sounds, and word sounds are repeated.

- Readability is determined by the number of words in each sentence, the number of characters in each word, and word lists based on curriculum frameworks.

- Full-color photography reinforces word meanings and concepts.

- "Words I Can Read" list at the end of each book teaches basic elements of grammar, helps the reader recognize the words in the text, and builds vocabulary.

- Reading levels are indicated by the number of flags on the castle.

Look for more SandCastle books in these three reading levels:

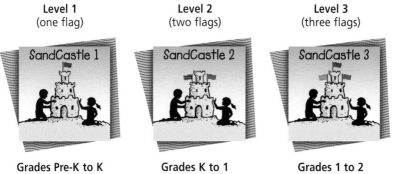

Level 1
(one flag)

Level 2
(two flags)

Level 3
(three flags)

Grades Pre-K to K
5 or fewer words per page

Grades K to 1
5 to 10 words per page

Grades 1 to 2
10 to 15 words per page

This is an exclamation point.

I know when to use exclamation points.

An **exclamation point** is used when something is exciting.

Eric caught a really big fish!

Paula can ride her bicycle very fast.

Look at her go!

!

John is thinking about
jumping off the diving
board.

It is a long way down!

Grace is getting a special prize from her teacher.

She is very proud!

I love to play baseball.

Maybe I will hit a
home run!

Wow! Look at my new doll!

I will name her Wanda.

Exclamation points show
that someone is yelling.

"Hey everybody! The ice
cream truck is coming!"

What does Tammy say
when she goes down
the slide?

("Whee!")

Words I Can Read

Nouns

A noun is a person, place, or thing

baseball (BAYSS-bawl)
p. 15
bicycle (BYE-si-kuhl) p. 9
diving board
(DIVE-ing BORD) p. 11
doll (DOL) p. 17

exclamation point
(ek-skluh-MAY-shuhn
POINT) pp. 5, 7
exclamation points
(ek-skluh-MAY-shuhn
POINTSS) pp. 5, 19
fish (FISH) p. 7
home run (HOME RUHN)
p. 15

ice cream truck
(EYESS KREEM TRUHK)
p. 19
prize (PRIZE) p. 13
slide (SLIDE) p. 21
teacher (TEECH-ur) p. 13
way (WAY) p. 11

Proper Nouns

A proper noun is the name of a person, place, or thing

Eric (ER-ik) p. 7
Grace (GRAYSS) p. 13

John (JON) p. 11
Paula (PAW-luh) p. 9

Tammy (TAM-ee) p. 21
Wanda (WON-duh) p. 17

Pronouns

A pronoun is a word that replaces a noun

everybody
(EV-ree-buh-dee) p. 19
her (HUR) pp. 9, 17
I (EYE) pp. 5, 15, 17

it (IT) p. 11
she (SHEE) pp. 13, 21
someone (SUHM-wuhn)
p. 19

something (SUHM-thing)
p. 7
this (THISS) p. 5
what (WUHT) p. 21

22

Verbs

A verb is an action or being word

can (KAN) p. 9
caught (KAWT) p. 7
coming (KUHM-ing) p. 19
does (DUHZ) p. 21
getting (GET-ing) p. 13
go (GOH) p. 9
goes (GOHZ) p. 21
hit (HIT) p. 15

is (IZ) pp. 5, 7, 11, 13, 19
jumping (JUHMP-ing) p. 11
know (NOH) p. 5
look (LUK) pp. 9, 17
love (LUHV) p. 15
name (NAYM) p. 17
play (PLAY) p. 15
ride (RIDE) p. 9

say (SAY) p. 21
show (SHOH) p. 19
teacher (TEECH-ur) p. 13
thinking (THINGK-ing) p. 11
use (YOOZ) p. 5
used (YOOZD) p. 7
will (WIL) pp. 15, 17
yelling (YEL-ing) p. 19

Adjectives

An adjective describes something

big (BIG) p. 7
exciting (ek-SITE-ing) p. 7
fast (FAST) p. 9

her (HUR) pp. 9, 13
long (LAWNG) p. 11
my (MYE) p. 17

new (NOO) p. 17
proud (PROUD) p. 13
special (SPESH-uhl) p. 13

Adverbs

An adverb tells how, when, or where something happens

maybe (MAY-bee) p. 15

really (REE-lee) p. 7

very (VER-ee) pp. 9, 13

Glossary

bicycle – a vehicle with two wheels, a seat, handlebars to steer with, and pedals that you push with your feet

diving board – a long wooden or plastic platform that sticks out over the end of a swimming pool so you can jump or dive off of it into the water

everybody – all of the people

home run – a hit in baseball that allows the batter to go around all of the bases and score

prize – a reward for doing something well or winning a competition or game

slide – a type of playground equipment with a smooth, slanted surface you sit on to ride down